THE LIFE

ALSO BY CARRIE FOUNTAIN

POETRY

Instant Winner (2014)

Burn Lake (2010)

FICTION

I'm Not Missing (2018)

THE LIFE

CARRIE
FOUNTAIN

PENGUIN POETS

PENGUIN BOOKS

An imprint of Penguin Random House LLC
penguinrandomhouse.com

LIBRARY OF CONGRESS CATALOGING-IN-PUBLICATION DATA
Names: Fountain, Carrie, author.
Title: The life / Carrie Fountain.
Description: [New York] : Penguin Books, [2021] | Series: Penguin poets
Identifiers: LCCN 2020043386 (print) | LCCN 2020043387 (ebook) | ISBN 9780143136019 (trade paperback) | ISBN 9780525507635 (ebook)
Subjects: LCGFT: Poetry.
Classification: LCC PS3606.O84425 L1 2021 (print) | LCC PS3606.O84425 (ebook) | DDC 811/.6—dc23
LC record available at https://lccn.loc.gov/2020043386
LC ebook record available at https://lccn.loc.gov/2020043387

Printed in the United States of America

1st Printing

Set in Sabon Lt Std
Designed by Catherine Leonardo

for K & O & J

But somewhere there is an ancient enmity
between our daily life and the great work.
Help me, in saying it, to understand it.

—RILKE

CONTENTS

II

ACKNOWLEDGMENTS

Some of these poems, a few with different titles, were first published in the following journals, magazines, newspapers, and anthologies, to whose editors my very grateful acknowledgment is made:

The Academy of American Poets Poem-a-Day
The American Poetry Review
Borderlands: Texas Poetry Review
EcoTheo Review
Gulf Coast
The Houston Chronicle
Image Magazine
Langdon Review
The New Yorker
Northwest Review
Poetry Northwest
The San Antonio Express-News
Texas Poetry Calendar
Upstreet

"First," "The End" (as "The End of the Year"), "Poem Without an Image," and "Aubade of the Three-Day Weekend," *Other Musics: New Latina Poetry,* ed. Cynthia Cruz, University of Oklahoma Press, 2019.

"Time to be the fine line of light" and "Poem from a Hotel

Room on Christmas Morning" (as "Christmas Morning in a Hotel Room"), *The Southern Poetry Anthology, Volume VIII,* ed. William Wright, Texas Review Press, 2018.

"Poem Without an Image," *The Long Devotion: Poets Writing Motherhood*, ed. Emily Pérez and Nancy Reddy, University of Georgia Press, 2021.

Thanks to Paul Slovak and Allie Merola at Penguin. Your care with this book has meant everything.

Thanks to Emily Forland, my friend who became my agent, and to Anya Backlund and Blue Flower Arts.

The love and friendship of many lit my way toward this book. Susannah Benson, Naomi Shihab Nye, Tomás Morín, Rebecca McInroy, Carra Martinez, Margo Rabb, Karen LaShelle, Deb Esquinazi, Clair Homan, Billie and Al Fountain, the women of Women's Group (we never did find a better name, did we?), the women of Book Club(ish), the women of afterschool concrete at Russell Lee Elementary: thank you.

Without the work of gifted childcare givers and teachers I would not have written this or any other book. Thank you. Fatima Osorio, your care and spirit continue to guide me. Thank you, friend.

Kirk Lynn: my life's love, my empowering partner. Thank you.

O and J: you are my life's greatest gifts. This book is for you.

THE LIFE

I

THE END

Hanging the miniature ornaments
on the miniature tree with the girl

while the baby sleeps behind a sheet
of white noise and uncorrupted

darkness. *Ow*, she says each time
the needles prick her fingers. Ow.

There is no way the little tree can
wear it all, can bear it all; its branches

begin to droop under the cheer, angels
mostly. Now the girl goes to bed

reluctantly, falls asleep instantly.
Now the night comes full on. And so,

in this way, the Christ child will be
born again, his animal life will begin

again, the story will begin again, his
tiny mouth will curl toward his mother's

breast, strong mouth of the newborn,
the part that comes knowing what

to do. They will meet for the first time.
She'll have those breasts until the end

of her life. He'll have that mouth until
the end of his.

THE LIFE

The toilet flows and flows
and nothing stops it

so I call a plumber but then
it stops on its own

so I call back and say it stopped
and cancel. I have these

little ideas for making my life
a marginally better life.

I can't think of one
right now. Otherwise, I find

as soon as I come within range
the spirit retreats. Before

long, it never existed. As with
a celebrity, I will always

have to remember meeting
the spirit, though the spirit will

never have to remember meeting
me. Based on conversations

I've overheard, I think
my children believe the soul

is an organ of the body.
I know they believe in heaven.

I hear them talk about it.
But theirs is a heaven of their own

making, a place where you can
do whatever you want, eat

ice cream for dinner, play
video games with a God who will

drive you to CVS—yes, right now,
put on your shoes—for a new box

of Lucky Charms, a God
who will give you full possession

of his Apple ID. Theirs
is a heaven with no elsewhere,

a heaven with no hell.
For them there are three times:

the beforelife, which is nothing,
the life, and the afterlife, which is

everything. Who knows? Maybe
they're right. If I washed

my face and brushed my teeth
and took out my contacts

right after putting my kids to sleep
rather than waiting until

before bed, my evenings would be
better and I'd go to sleep earlier.

There. You see, I can't stop having
the smallest possible ideas. This

is the life. After a day of devout
silence, the toilet starts up again.

This time I'm waiting to see
if it's serious.

POEM ON THE INSIDE

Writing in the silent
part of the morning, before

the baby and his toys
wake up and begin

their strange chatter,
the lawn mower's insipid

giggle, the cell phone's
hello and *goodbye*.

The only sound now is that
of the cat licking his fur

behind me on the bed.
In the short time after

we bought this house
but before we moved into it,

I'd sometimes drive by.
I'd stop. I'd park in the carport

and sneak around back
and I'd squint into the windows,

almost certain I knew what
our lives would be like

once we lived inside.

COLD

Wind through the night, cold
wind to blow the dried skins

away, maybe. We woke to find
the thousand yellow leaves

of the pecan tree covering
the backyard. What is

the meaning of this? the villain
in the show my children

are watching asks, his face to
the heavens. I think he's going to

turn good, my son says.
And I say, Hope so, because

I know how much he loves a bad guy
who just needs one experience

of goodness to turn good
himself—good again, finally

good, his evil so simple, just pain
and fear and shame, evil that begs

to be thwarted, to be finished,
solved, dissolved, like sugar

in water, no more next time, there
won't be a next time, because

the curse is lifted, the lesion healed,
the disease cured. We thought

he was dead in the end, but then
no—look, he's breathing, he's

alive, he lived. Any of us
could be turned inside out

like that, then right side in—any
one of us could suddenly run

a finger over the tender spot,
the crack that could widen then

break apart cleanly, moved by
love, destroyed by love, and replaced

by love, a force so strong, a wind
that blows cleanly through

the darkest night, a wind that blows
the dried skins away, until we rise

again, ready to account
for the damage we've done.

THE BEAST IS COMING

is what my daughter
said all through the first

part of the song, where
Belle is singing about how

surprised she is to be falling
in love with a beast: *The beast*

is coming, right, Mommy?
What a story. He is a beast,

a true beast, with fur and
haunches and claws that slash,

no metaphor, yellow teeth, very
bad attitude, yet a woman

still finds a way to love him.
It was alarming how easily

my girl gave over. *He's not so*
grumpy anymore, she said,

and look, he took a bath.

AFTER THE ASCENSION

No one wanted to look at each other.
No one wanted to speak, to be
the first to speak. But we had to.

Walking back to Jerusalem, for instance,
we had to decide where we were going.
There was no one to follow home

anymore. That day and the day after.
Waking, it was the first thought. *This*
is the feeling of rising with faith alone.

We had to learn it like a skill. We had
to come to understand this would always
be the first thought. Things hadn't

worked out the way we'd thought
they would. Eventually, we began dying.
Funny to say it now, but some of us

wondered, would it happen to us, too?
But of course it would happen. This was
the very promise we'd lived by.

ONE WAY

When I quit smoking it was only because
I'd come to understand without a doubt that
I was unable to quit smoking. I knew I could

not do it. I knew that if I wanted to not smoke
I'd have to maintain the specific circumstances
that would keep me from failing to quit

smoking, those specific circumstances being
that I not smoke. And it worked, which still
amazes me. When our daughter was a baby

and was learning to put herself to sleep
and was crying and crying—well, after a while
I would need to go into her room and make it

stop—*I just need to make it stop*—and the longer
it went on, the stronger was my need to make it
stop. *No*, my husband said. *She's wrestling*

with the devil, my husband said. *And we must
let her win.* Now I pray, when I pray, understanding
I cannot pray—*okay, fine*—and also understanding

the only way to quit not praying is to enter the arena
of prayer, lay hands upon the devil—my devil—and
pin it down as long as I can, then a while after that.

FIRST

There is a holiness in exhaustion,
is what I keep telling myself,
filling out the form so my TA gets paid,
then making copies of it on the hot
and heaving machine, writing
Strong start! on a pretty bad poem.
And then the children: the baby's
mouth opening, going for the breast,
the girl's hair to wash tonight
and then comb so painstakingly
in the tub while conditioner drips
in slick globs onto her shoulders
and her discipline chart flaps in the air
conditioner at school, taped
to a filing cabinet, longing for
stickers. My heart is so giant
this evening, like one of those moons
so full it's disturbing, so full that
if you see it when you're getting out
of the car you have to go inside the house
and make someone else come out
and see it for themselves. I want
everything, I admit. I want
a clean heart. I want the children
to sleep and the drought to end.
I want the rain to come down hard—
It's supposed to monsoon, is what

Naomi said, driving away this morning,
and she was right. It's monsooning.
Still I want more. Even as the streets
are washed clean and then begin
to flood. Even though the man came
again today to check the rat traps
and said he bet we'd catch the rat
within twenty-four hours. We still haven't
caught the rat, so I'm working
at the table with my legs folded up
beneath me. I want to know
what is holy—I do. But first I want
the rat to die. I am thirsty for that
death and will drink deeply of that
victory, the thwack of the trap's
hard plastic jaw, and I will rush
to see the evidence no matter how
gruesome, folding my body over
the washing machine to see the thing
crushed there, much smaller than
I imagined it'd be, the strawberry
large in its mouth.

HOW HAS MOTHERHOOD CHANGED THE WAY YOU WRITE?

The baby sleeps
and cries and sleeps

and cries in fifteen-
minute increments

for three hours
and wakes, unrested,

wanting something,
something I cannot

give him. Meanwhile
the sheets hold their

famous crumple,
their human scent.

Meanwhile, in the kitchen
the enchilada casseroles

wait in the freezer
for their big moment,

though casseroles
cannot wait

because casseroles
have no desires.

Look at the oranges
in the white bowl

on the table. Suddenly
they've been there

for weeks and have
hardened, been

rendered inedible,
despite appearances.

Suddenly a smell
comes strongly

from a hidden place
in the backyard

and we cannot
discover it and will

never discover it.
All we can do is say

Something died
out there every time

we go in or out the back
door. Suddenly it's deep

winter and the baby
has produced one crude

tooth and the trees
in front of the house

across the street
are bare of leaves

and the people we knew
have moved back

to Houston and the house
has been on the market

for going on three months.
One day, the blinds were

open all day and all
night, the empty house

emitting light, staged
by experts, soft

throws folded over
armchairs. Still,

no takers.

THE PARABLE OF THE GIFTS

My son can't keep the story straight.
Is he going to come into my room?

he asks his sister warily of Santa Claus.
He is so young he routinely needs to be

reminded what to believe. Santa is real;
aliens are not real. *Aliens could be real*,

my daughter says. *Yeah, I guess you're*

right, I say. *And Jesus Christ is real*,
she says. *Zeus wasn't real. Zeus was*

a myth. But Jesus Christ was a real man
who walked upon this earth though

he was the Son of God. So I guess
she's made it to the New Testament

in the *100 Bible Stories for Children* she bought
last week with her tooth fairy money.

Sure you want that one? her father asked
at the checkout, and as an answer

she held the book tightly to her chest.
God, sometimes I can see the privacy

forming around her, like faint light
or like the shimmer of oil as it heats

in the pan, and it is a great mystery
to me, and it is painful to me, because

it is lonely to be a person and what she is
telling us with her 100 Bible stories

is that she is a person. God, sometimes I step
into this life like stepping into a room

I can't remember why I entered, and for
a moment I see nothing—I can see nothing,

I can see it, a space in front of me that is not yet
filled, that could be filled, and will be filled.

It's simple and elegant, without needs, just
large enough, and sometimes I understand

that's the space my babies came from, were
pulled from wailing, and the space

my grandmother returned to, finally, after
her long and painful illness, but suddenly, too,

that morning, with the scent of orange
Jell-O still present in the room, she slipped

away, was pulled, perhaps, and I imagine
that's the space I'll enter, too, when I die,

and it's not unpleasant to think of it,
an ultimate privacy, though thinking

of my children with spaces of their own
into which they will someday disappear

is unbearable. It is unbearable, and though
it is unbearable, I bear it. That is the agreement

into which I entered when they arrived.
I think maybe I should read ahead to see

how the book handles the Crucifixion.
Or maybe I should just hide the book

and pretend I didn't. *I don't know. I haven't*
seen it. Maybe the tooth fairy will bring you

more money and you can buy something else.
Because, God, I am not prepared to let

my daughter know how the main character
of her story dies. Not yet. She, who answers

her brother so kindly, with such perfect
honesty, saying, *No, the gifts just appear*

under the tree; it's magic, though surely
by now she only pretends to believe.

THE STUDENT

I wish I were as talented
at anything as he is

at pulling Derrida into
a conversation, any

conversation, no matter
what we're discussing:

Derrida. Even once
when he was telling me

why he didn't have
the assignment, even then

after a long and aerobic
journey we arrived

at Derrida, his white
hair and elegant European

ideas, and it felt good—
I admit it felt good to finally

arrive there—*ah, bonjour,*
Monsieur Derrida!—

because at least I knew
then where I was, even

if it wasn't where
I wanted to be. *To pretend,*

Derrida said, *I actually*
do the thing: I have therefore

only pretended to pretend.
I pretend sometimes. Other

times all I do is pretend.
I've created gods this way

and on occasion I've tied
those gods together

like they do bedsheets
in a movie, and I've escaped

the high tower of myself
this way. I've made it

to solid ground this way.
I've landed on the earth.

And each time I've been
sure I've actually done

the thing, but when I look up,
the gods are gone.

MASHA EVENTUALLY

After the Russian folktale "Masha and the Bear"

At first, I couldn't decide
if I should call the bear *it*

or if I should call the bear *him.*
At first, this distinction

was important to me,
and because it was a problem

I could solve entirely within
my own body, I worked on it

daily, like a chore, until
everything inside me

was arranged in neat columns:
pile of clean laundry, stack

of clean dishes. I'd gotten myself
into this mess, I could hear

my grandmother saying
from her own reprehensible

century. Now I'd pay the price
of my girlhood, as all women

must. Okay, I thought. Maybe
this is a rite of passage.

I was, after all, a woman
in the eyes of the bear. And so

in the eyes of the bear I tried
to find the moral of my story.

But I never did. I never could.
Too often I blacked out,

the pain and fear ripping
through my woman's body,

exposing the girl's bones
beneath, the girl's blood,

upon which the ships
of this world had for so long

been kept afloat. The sun
coming through the clean

windows in the morning
was still sometimes enough

to make me glow with
happiness. But even that

became disgusting, eventually:
that weakness in me, that

beauty. One evening I checked
to see if the problem was

solved, but found I couldn't
remember why I'd cared

to solve it. The answer
had slipped from my grasp.

One moment I was beating
the rugs, coming to

a conclusion; the next I was
washing the teapot, thinking

of exactly nothing.
That's when I knew it

didn't matter. The bear was
an *it*—a dumb thing with

needs and teeth, a thing
into the hand of which

I could climb and from which
I could stay hidden if it didn't

find me and eat me first,
bone and blood, hair

and clothing. I liked
so much imagining the look

of wonder on my grandmother's
face when she opened the door

to see me there, returned.
I took my chances.

POEM MADE OF REVISIONS

The hot-air balloon hanging over
the now-distant mesa of my childhood

was something else before; it was
the ultra-fat wrists of my babies,

maybe, the creases where flesh met
flesh and sometimes, impossibly,

met flesh again, and before that
it was a confession, or was it a brag

revised into a confession, that once
or twice I've fallen deeply in love

with someone I made up entirely
in my imagination, and that one time

it turned out the one I'd made up
was living in the body of a man I did not

love, and yet sometimes when I slept
with that man there'd come a moment

when I'd feel this great disorienting
displeasure—or was it pleasure?—

as the real one gave way, shook and fell
beneath the weight of my love

for the made-up one, until the real one
was nothing, dust that blew away

from me, which was fine because
it turned out he was a dipshit, and now

it's the last time I walked over the bridge
into Juárez with my cousins, to drink

at the Kentucky Club the night before
my grandfather's funeral, and how

sitting in that booth, looking toward
the bar in smoky light, it felt like

we'd snuck into another time,
my grandfather's time, when he'd

drive to Juárez to buy produce
for his restaurant, stop at the Kentucky

Club for a drink, and then, on the way
back into America, would have to park

and get out and sit at the border
and slice open each avocado, remove

the seed, throw it away, and then
carefully put the two pieces

back together again, all under
the watchful eye of some customs

agent, and I remember that night
so vividly, maybe because I know now

what we didn't know then: that it'd be
the last time we'd walk across

that bridge like that, together, and how
the next day, at the funeral, a dove

hit the window above the altar
with a great thump just as the priest

began the heated whispering
that accompanies the preparation

of the host, and that he never
looked up—he never even looked up—

and I have for all these years
imagined the attention he gave

to the body and blood of his savior
was for him so real—so immaculate

and so very real—as to be
impenetrable, and that he believed

that if he stopped even for a moment
he'd lose the thread of his faith,

and break the promise he'd made
and believed in, which was the gist

of his lifetime's work: making one
thing become another.

SELF-HELP

Your thoughts and feelings
are natural, there, like air,
and like air you can improve
or degrade them, but you
cannot make them. You do
not make the air. Congratulations,
you can say every morning
to your thoughts and feelings.
You made it, you survived
the night. You're back.
Your poems are not your work.
Poems are art and art is not
work, not exactly, though art
is made of work. Poems
are made of work. Once,
I stopped the work. That's when
and how I learned about the work.
The work is nothing like air.
It's more like looking up now
to see my son's small shoulder
and his arm slid palm-up under
the pillow, his ear pushed out
from under his wild hair. It's like
this—like the way I'm writing
quietly at my chair in the dark
this morning, drinking coffee
I make in my closet, watching him

sleep in my bed, which he came into
last night, guided as he is after eight p.m.
entirely by his fears, especially
his fear of waking in the night
to find himself alone, a fear I read
about last night while he slept
beside me, a fear experts say
I should accept rather than encourage
to go away. *No one ever bootstrapped*
their way out of fear, one article
said, and it struck me as so true
and so obvious that I had to wait
a while for the wave of shame
to wash over me, for of course
I'd been pushing hard for
independence. I've read enough
advice from experts to have
learned one thing: that you have to
let the shame come—parenting
is full of shame and the recognition
of shame and the legacy
of shame—and you have to let it
come and wash over you
without trying to stop it. I read
that the best thing to do is accept
your child's fear, accept it all,
be there with him in it, share it, tend

to it like you would a minor wound.
People always have advice, but
hardly any people are experts.
And so today we'll be changing
gears. From now on we're going to
be there with him in his fear.
Which is work. Now, it's later
and both kids are up and my son
is long gone, the blankets
tossed, the sun up, his sister
up, his fears burned off like
fog, and he is making an absurd
amount of noise in the living room
while his sister, who is too old
to do so, is lying on the floor
trying to engage me in an argument
about whether this room or her room
is the biggest carpeted room
in the house. *I'm working, baby,*
I tell her, though by now I've long
lost the thread of this work, and she
gets up reluctantly and skulks
out of the room. For a while I listen
to the two of them talking
down the hall. *Do you like this little*
place I made for my Tamagotchi?
and *So what? Even though the airport*

isn't moving, it gives me motion sickness! and *There's something I always say and that is, McDonald's makes me McDonald's sick*. Congratulations, I say to myself, right here, right now on this page, in this moment. *Yeah, you're really good. You could probably become a cat hairstylist*. You made it.

THE ANSWER

When my son cried out
in the night I woke—ready—

and scrambled to his room
without even putting on

my glasses, pulled through
the dark living room and down

the dark hall by this instinct
I'm still sometimes surprised

to possess. By the time
I got to him he'd fallen back

to sleep, of course, and so there
I was, awake, squinting down

on him, twisted up in Paw
Patrol sheets, his body emitting

that constant low heat of the still-
growing. What a miracle,

I thought then, that I'll always
get to recall the slant look

he gave me when the nurse
first brought his new face up

to mine and I could see even
then, from the start, he was

sizing me up, finding me
somewhere in the adequate-

to-lacking range, though
he must've known—must've

come knowing—that I'd
have to do. Trying to untangle

him from the sheets, I woke
him, of course, and he looked up

at me, mystified, my face
inches from his. When he asked

what I was doing there,
I answered, *I'm not here, go*

back to sleep, and he did.
Once, my life was neat.

It was a handkerchief, folded,
slipped into a back pocket.

No one had to know
it was even there. Now,

it's opened. And wasn't it
this I prayed for in some

distant, quiet place, all
alone, all lonesome and alone?

Wasn't it God I asked
to allow me the grace

to one day learn the names
of all the dogs on *Paw Patrol*,

all the ponies on *My Little
Pony*, all the Pokémon, good

and bad, the Care Bears,
the Transformers, the enemies

of Batman, the friends of
Batman, all the good guys

and all the bad guys forever
and ever, amen? *Make it*

real. Wasn't that exactly
what I'd asked for?

THE JUNGLE

In motherhood I begin
to celebrate my own

smallest accomplishments,
as when I wake to find

I've slept through the night
and I feel a little healed

because sleeping is something
I didn't learn how to do until

I was an adult and had to read
a book about it because, I've

always liked to joke, I was
raised by wolves. *I was raised*

by wolves was, in fact, the very
joke I made in explaining

to a fellow mom as the children's
theater went dark that, like my own

young son, I was seeing *The Jungle*
Book for the first time. I don't

even know what it's about, I said.
I was sort of raised by wolves,

I said, and laughed, and then
the curtain went up and I was

shocked, of course, to find
The Jungle Book is about a boy

who was raised by wolves,
and I am shocked again now,

having just googled it, to find
the number one query

associated with Rudyard
Kipling is, *Is* The Jungle Book

a real story? People are dumb,
is what I was thinking, I admit,

when I read that, but then
I clicked and clicked and found

that—oh my god—*The Jungle*
Book is based on the story

of a feral boy found running
on all fours alongside a wolf

in the Indian jungle, which is
funny to me because *feral*

is the word that has always come
to mind when I think of the boys

I grew up with: those feral boys
who moved through the world

with the ease afforded to those
who didn't give two shits

about anything, who'd empty
beer cans in seconds, wrap cars

around poles, all the while joking
about fucking each other's

mothers. They were feral
in the desert, shooting guns out

by the airport. They were feral
on their skateboards in the Whata-

burger parking lot. They were feral
because they were allowed

to be, and eventually we'd all
get in trouble for what they'd been

doing, even us girls who—what did
we do all that time while the boys

were fighting and spitting
and calling us whores? I don't

know. We were talking to each
other, I guess, which is how we

became human. But no—no.
Those boys weren't feral. Those boys

were typical. They'd been born
knowing the world would be theirs

long after they'd grown bored
of nihilism and turned their attention

to capital, became men, became man-
kind, the kind of men who'd ruin

something if it meant they got to
keep it, who'd kill something

if it meant they could see it up close,
maintain the illusion of having

owned it, having earned it, even,
who'd track a boy and a wolf

through the jungle for days until
finally they had them trapped

inside their own den. When those
men found they couldn't lure

the boy out with words, they forced
him out with smoke. And when

the boy finally stepped out into
the sunlight those men captured

him, bound him, and when the wolf
who was the boy's mother came

following close behind, the way,
at intermission, I followed my own

young son, who is by now too old
to come with me into the women's

room, to the very threshold
of the men's room door—when she

came out behind him, they shot her.

II

POEM WITH A DREAM OF THE FUTURE IN IT

I hear my children speaking
with their future shrinks.

One says, *It was as if whining*
was a war crime and I was

always on trial. The other
remembers this one time

his mother made him cry
asking him to stop playing

with his penis so she could
close the diaper around it

and put him to bed. There
are others in there, too, to bear

witness: the woman
at the picnic who scolded me

for spraying Off! on my toddler's
toes, asking through a mouth

full of potato salad, *You don't*
want to poison this little angel,

do you? And the man who
approached me in the bulk foods

section at the co-op during
the last week of my first

pregnancy to ask if I'd have
the baby in the hospital

or at home, and then, when
I said hospital, went off about

the evils of Western medicine,
right there, surrounded by

the silent nuts and grains
and many kinds of silent rice:

he is there to testify that
I, too, was silent, that I did not

tell him to shut up, seek help,
fuck off, that I probably even

said thank you before
I finally maneuvered my cart

around him and escaped.
She was never brave enough,

I hear my grown daughter
say. *It took her too long*

to recognize how deeply
she'd internalized the patriarchy,

and even longer before she did
anything about it. She wrote

poems about us and then,
when people asked her if

that really happened, *she'd get*
angry and say we were

metaphors. I wait in the hall.
I pace. I skim an article

containing dire warnings
about the future in *Time*

magazine. I can't help
myself. I peer through

the keyhole. The scene. Those
I tried so hard to love

correctly. The wars I fought
I thought were the right

wars, the sides I took I believed
were the right sides.

And the shrink, nodding,
furiously writing notes.

I cannot see what she is
writing, not even here,

in my own dream. This,
too, I must let happen.

SHORT POEM WITH INSOMNIA

Sometimes it's not the act
but the idea of sleep that

slips, one end of a knot
falling away from the other,

the sack billowing open.
Then, it's the self who's left

to watch, unable to reconcile
her own lack of ability in this

effort. We can do almost
anything by will, even the worst

things. But we cannot will
ourselves to sleep. And so this

enmity emerges in the night
between the deliberate self

and the other, the one who,
for whatever reason, cannot

or will not be coaxed, not even
once, to show her perfect face.

SUMMERTIME

I flush the latest dead fish down
the toilet before the children
come home. We bought the fish
to be little responsibility lessons
and then little death lessons
for the children, though the fish
keep dying for no clear reason
and somehow I am the only one
who is ever home to partake
of the death lessons. The children
are at camp learning to be bored
and itchy with a few moments
of wonder and one to two friends
each. They are having childhoods
and I am having adulthood,
watching the silver body that just
this morning contained a life
flash like money one last time
before vanishing down the drain,
trying to decide whether or not
to tell them when they arrive,
their faces red from sun and chlorine.
I pray here, over the toilet, that in
the moment, I will tell them the truth
and that I will tell it well enough.

POEM MAKING CHANGE

The computer was cold, but now
it's warm in my lap, and the girl

made it through the night without
ambling into our bedroom, complaining

of some imaginary ailment suffered
by her Glow Pet. So, yes. So why not

be fine for five minutes, even if there
is no reason in the world to be fine,

even if just last week in the parking lot
of the grocery store someone wrote

FUCK U in the dust on the side
of your car, beneath the window where

the baby sits in his laudably safe
car seat, looking out onto the world,

wordless, with the true concern
and puzzlement of the wholly innocent?

Why not get up right now and do what
you keep telling yourself you've been

meaning to do for days: go out there
right now and get rid of it. Go get

your own hands dirty wiping it away.

POEM WITHOUT AN IMAGE

Just now it has come
to me again: the sudden
knowledge of everything
that remains to be done
though I worked my ass off
this week, doing things, doing
things. *What is my style?*
is a question I have never
asked until now, in the waiting
room at my dentist's,
when this article in O magazine
encouraged me so cunningly
to do so. Maybe it is not
my job to surprise you, not
anymore, says the spirit.
OK, I say. OK. But still,
I want one more crisp
image, just one, though I know
I don't deserve it, I want it
to appear the way money once
or twice in my life has appeared
in my line of vision on
the street: some bill, nearly
alive, green god, its skin
giving off evergreen light,
unaccounted for and then
immediately mine, no
questions asked.

WILL YOU?

When, at the end, the children wanted
to add glitter to their valentines, I said no.

I said, *Nope, no, no glitter*, and then,
when they started to fuss, I found myself

saying something my brother's football coach
used to bark from the sidelines when one

of his players showed signs of being
human: *Oh, come on now, suck it up.*

That's what I said to my children.
Suck what up? my daughter asked,

and because she is so young, I told her
I didn't know and never mind, and she took

that for an answer. My children are so young
when I turn off the radio as the news turns

to counting the dead or naming the act,
they aren't even suspicious. My children

are so young they cannot imagine a world
like the one they live in. Their God is still

a real God, a whole God, a God made wholly
of actions. And I think they think I work

for that God. And I know they will someday soon
see everything and they will know about

everything and they will no longer take
never mind for an answer. The valentines

would've been better with glitter, and my son
hurt himself on an envelope, and then, much

later, when we were eating dinner, my daughter
realized she'd forgotten one of the three

Henrys in her class. *How can there be three Henrys
in one class?* I said, and she said, *Because there are.*

And so, before bed we took everything out
again—paper and pens and stamp and scissors—

and she sat at the table with her freshly washed hair
parted smartly down the middle and wrote,

WILL YOU BE MINE, HENRY T.? and she did it
so carefully, I could hardly stand to watch.

THE QUESTION OF YOUR YOUTH

You lost it when you were
young, but you didn't know

you were young. All the people
you'd left, you could still

make out their faces, would
know their phone numbers

by heart for many years,
would carry the weird secrets

they'd told you, which felt
so heavy at the time, deep

into your own life, long after
their potency had expired.

You can still recall them now
with the same wonder and

gravity: *HM's father was drunk*
at midnight mass and peed in

the parking lot at Holy Cross.
JB had sex with the girls'

volleyball coach, but they
were IN LOVE. You'd stayed

in your hometown too long.
You hadn't cared enough

about getting into a good
college until long after college

when you found yourself
surrounded by people who'd

gone to good colleges. The idea
of escaping hadn't carried

the same glory for you as it had
for others, some who were so

eager to go they'd seemed
to vanish into the future, gone

suddenly and forever. You were
a late bloomer, but you wouldn't

know that until it was too late.
What is this life for, anyway?

That was the question of your
youth. You thought you'd discard it

once you'd arrived at an answer.
But you never arrived, and so

you kept hold of the question
as it pulled you along—single you,

little you—as it had from
the beginning, down through

the birth canal, through the heavy
sawdust smell of childhood

where your mother's jar of sun
tea sat darkening forever outside

the front door, into the hotel room
where you found a single sock

under the bed and felt
for a moment that uncanny

feeling that you had truly
glimpsed someone else's life,

into the grocery store, where just
earlier today you pushed

your cart up and down the aisles,
reading labels, worrying

about how much sugar
you feed your children.

It's a relief, isn't it, to see it
when you see it, when for

whatever reason you're allowed
to see it: the question of your

youth, always exactly where
you least expect to see it, yours,

yes, distinctly so, but by now
knotted up with so many others

that it is unable to be extracted,
taken away, finally—finally—

unable to be answered.

DOMESTIC AUBADE

It was you who made me
sit admiring the reflection

of our newly mown lawn
in our neighbor's newly

clean windows. It was you
who asked me to try—*just*

try—discerning the deeper
meanings while our girl

turned up the Barbie music
full blast so that within

the sanctity of her pink
bedroom she could perfect

her moves. It was you
who said, *There's your*

holy business right
there. You asked me to go

back and describe the grass
slung in pulverized clumps

all over the underside
of the lawnmower, still

wet, such a bright
and tender green. Once

I confided in you that
I wanted to make soup

and pay the cable bill
forever while the baby

napped inside his drowsy
cloud of swaddles beside me

on the sofa. I was worried
that was all I'd ever want.

Just go for it, you said. And so
I went for it. I went forward.

I took it all and keep
taking it. It was you who

taught me to want. Now,
I want.

after children.
after a nervous breakdown.
after fifty/sixty/seventy.
after your double mastectomy.

while cheating on your spouse.
while impotent.
while going through the change.
while divorced.

instead of divorce.
instead of misery.
instead of living on the tips of others.
instead of an unhappy marriage.

when the children have grown and left, just as you always
suspected they wouldn't.
when the streaks on your windshield catch the sunset
and blind you.
when your daughter stares out the window in the back seat, an
other being, afloat on the raft of her growing body in an ocean
of thoughts you will never know, and fears, surely, and
frightening sadnesses you can know and will still never be able
to do anything about.

when you think you might be dying.
when your spouse doesn't believe you're dying.
when you know you're dying.

despite—
forever—

for the children.
in space.
in America.
in a microhouse.

throughout.

double blinded.
halfway.

on the way.

even after.
and even after that.

LULLABY AFTER BEDTIME

We kick the dog out and lock the door
and make love quietly. *You locked*

the door, yes? I ask, and you answer,
Yes, from between my legs. *I locked*

the door. Later, the dog comes back in
and resumes her hesitant repose

while we watch a *Queer Eye.*
The children sleep and the cats

groom themselves sleepily. Another
day, blown over to rest atop the pile

of finished days. Eventually,
in the past, it will be tonight, and all

the nights like this night I will find
difficult to remember in the future,

difficult to recall anything in particular,
though it's all so vivid to me now:

the bad light bulb flickering in from
the bathroom, the coffee stain on

the nightstand, you falling asleep
saying *I think I'm falling asleep,*

and me saying, *Let's pause it here.*
We can watch the rest tomorrow.

Before sleep, along that private path
that leads to sleep, I resume once again

the fight I've been having for some
years now in my mind with the poet

who never changed, refused to change,
and then died, and in the dream

that follows, I'm once again wearing
a heavy sweater in the heat

of the desert trailing a pack of men
who drop trash which I pick up and put

in my pockets. Without even waking,
there, in the dream itself, where I have

stopped to watch the men get farther
and farther away, I will understand

what the sweater represents and I'll
wake up sweating and ashamed.

How could it never have occurred
to me until now to simply take off

that cumbersome garment? I suppose
it was because I believed the garment

was my skin. That was part of my sin.
I account for it here. I am not dead yet.

POEM WITH OUR MARRIAGE IN IT

Remember when the couple in that Chagall started floating off over the thatched roofs of their biscuit-colored village into the big, blue nostril of the day, holding hands and smiling? In the museum that afternoon you kept handing me Kleenex you begged from strangers because something about Paris was making me sneeze and cough and weep from one eye. *Maybe it's the romance*, you said. Now we know that we hardly knew each other then. We've only now begun to understand the sky is a very long story—you tell it or I tell it, doesn't matter. It's ours. Eventually, in the painting, the night will come. The man and the woman will look down to see that far below them on an otherwise empty street in a city they visited only once and now long ago, a rooster in a bow tie is playing a fiddle with no strings simply for the pleasure of hearing himself do it.

It was in the shoe I found
on the sidewalk outside
the school yesterday, still
warm inside. After I held it
up as if to attract its owner
and no one claimed it
and no one in sight was
missing a shoe, I put it
down, left it where I'd
found it, and when my son,
who is always feeling
these days for the edges
of things, said, *That's*
littering, I said, *Come on,*
no, it's not. Childhood is so
perfect, the way the rules,
if unbent, can bear
the weight of the structure
and protect the little creatures
still forming inside it.
We don't say "perfect," your
daughter, the perfectionist,
would remind you. *We say*
"good enough." Right. Right,
I taught her that. How good
enough: to know nothing

is hiding, to know there is
no secret message just for you
to discern, there is nothing
holding it all together,
nothing binding the known
and the unknown and
the unknowable, or not.

between the blind and the sill, nothing
really. There are so many things

that destroy. To think solely of them
is as foolish and expedient as not

thinking of them at all. All I want
is to be the river, though I return

again and again to the clouds.
All I want is to stop beginning sentences

with *All I want*. No—no, really, all
I want is this morning: my daughter

and my son saying *Da!* back and forth
over breakfast, cracking each other up

while eating peanut butter toast
and raspberries, making a place for

the two of them I will, eventually,
no longer be allowed to enter. Time to be

the fine line. Time to practice being
the line. And then, maybe, the darkness.

says the heart that feels itself lost in a world
of hearts, unknown by others. Excuse me,

says the body. Feed me, says the child. Feed
me what? says the mother. Feed me, please,

says the child. That's better. Today the world
will open as it does every day, and that scrim

behind which you hide—you will push at it.
You will try. Someday it will give way.

And what will you find looking back
at you? Who will your true audience be?

MY OWN AMERICAN POEM

O this flesh, this moment
passing, this sense that if

I don't get it done now
it won't get done. And it

won't get done. *I'm TCB,*
I text my husband when

I'm humming down
my to-do list, signing our

kids up for sports
they'll hate and camps

that will give them poison
ivy when all they'd

really like to do is watch
TV and make guns

out of Legos all summer,
be idle and free

and twisted, the way
we were in the good old

days. Of course, the good
old days were a lie.

I grew up believing Elvis
was king of the good

old days before our good
old days and he died

exhausted by a life of
privilege, on the toilet,

the king on his throne,
lost to the world

in the most idle place
in Graceland. I think

the most American
thing I do is waste

time: American both
to think of time as

something to use
and American to fail

to use it. Last night,
the swift, bitter cold

of climate change froze
the cactus, but this morning

the sunrise reflected back
the smoke of a distant

forest fire. A real stunner.
My problem is I am not

good the way poets are
supposed to be good.

I look at the night sky
and only want one more

chance to find the boots
I saw at Nordstrom

and didn't buy. We have
a sitter, is what I want to yell

into the night, victorious,
when we have a sitter.

I don't know. I no longer
wish to live by the laws

of coincidence. Yet, otherwise,
I struggle to find meaning.

I have nothing to teach
by word or example.

I have no good stories,
no good ideas, and if I did

I wouldn't want to share
them with you in a competition

of words and images. Or maybe
I would, but only if I win.

POEM FROM A HOTEL ROOM ON CHRISTMAS MORNING

Out the window, the parking lot
and the highway beyond it, going
off, going out. No doubt something
important began or ended there, or
there, or there—right out there, in
the spot where the white rental car
is right now idling, clouds of exhaust
billowing up like hope, like the precise
hope of the Christ child, silent in his
mother's arms, finally silent after
the great yanking commotion of birth.
Mother Mary, full of adrenaline, her
most radiant and successful self, smelling
her baby's head, touching his cheek
with the back of her finger. *Finally,*
you're here. Finally, you've arrived.
The frost on the car's windshield begins
to burn off in triangles where the heater
hits it. The stranger's face remains
obscured behind the wheel, just as
my face likewise remains hidden
from the stranger. All I can see
is the back seat, piled high with gifts.

TO WHITE NOISE

You are the sound silence
makes in its sleep, air made

visible by smoke, deepest
breath with no breathing,

O my personal ocean, O un-
broken *shush* of mortality,

O my digital sister, thank
you, thank you for keeping

the children from climbing
over the fence of sleep.

THE VOICE

Outside Dublin, Texas, the radio stations
disappear and I'm left alone with the faint
voice of a call-in psychologist talking
to a man in Cleveland about the voice
of the self, the narratives that voice
tells, how they can be sharp and wrong
and cut to the bone—whose bone? I don't
know. It's hard for me to imagine being
human, even at this late a date, and it's
impossible to know with certainty that
within my own chest there pumps a heart
the size of my fist. The narrative of the man
on the radio is so foreign to me—he lost
money going into business with a friend
and is angry and vengeful and resistant
to the advice of the nice psychologist,
which I immediately ascribe to misogyny.
And yet his voice—the voice he speaks
with—is so tender, so familiar. We're here
so briefly, the voice under his words says,
and we see so dimly; awful things have
happened to us, or will; we love our children
more than we are equipped to love anyone,
would die or kill for them, and we love
our own people even after they hurt us,
sometimes even more then, and yet we fail

at loving our neighbor; our only true weapon
is empathy and we fail again and again to use
it; and the one and only reason we must
love this inadequate world is because we have
no other choice, we have no other place
but this place, this earth and water where
our ancestors once moved across continents
and oceans, conquering or being conquered, so
alive—so alive with all their love and all their
hate, moving forward, just like us, unable to
imagine that one day they'd be ancestors.

This is the life with fried eggs.
This is the life with Pyrex dishes

of many sizes, none of which
I purchased myself. This is the life

with the boy who'd eat chicken
nuggets for every meal and the girl

who's asked four times this week
if she can please clean the cat's ears

again with a Q-tip. They are dirty.
No, they're not. This is the life

with lives in it so small we have to
put up a sign on the front door—

DON'T FORGET THE FISH—or
we'd forget the fish. This life:

sometimes I feel myself so deep
inside it, blessed so painfully, so

painfully blessed, pushing into it,
pushing—and yet I cannot

get through. I want too much.
I want a God who will save us all

and a God who will feel the little heat
coming off the candle I lit in the grotto.

A God in heaven, but a God here,
too, you know? I want a God like

the one I tell my children about, the one
who loves everyone. Even Trump? Well,

I guess so, yes. Even Trump. Please
give me a God that exists. That's all

I'll ever want. And the spirit says,
OK. And I say, Really? And the spirit

says, Yeah. Probably. Yeah.

JESSICA ATTIE

CARRIE FOUNTAIN's poems have appeared in *Tin House*, *Poetry*, and *The New Yorker*, among others. She is the author of the poetry collections *Burn Lake* (2010), a National Poetry Series winner, and *Instant Winner* (2014), along with the young adult novel *I'm Not Missing* (2018) and the children's book *The Poem Forest* (2022). Born and raised in Mesilla, New Mexico, Fountain received her MFA as a fellow at the James A. Michener Center for Writers at the University of Texas at Austin. She lives between Austin and rural southern New Mexico with her husband, playwright and novelist Kirk Lynn, and their two children.

PENGUIN POETS

GAROUS ABDOLMALEKIAN
Lean Against This Late Hour

PAIGE ACKERSON-KIELY
Dolefully, A Rampart Stands

JOHN ASHBERY
Selected Poems
Self-Portrait in a Convex Mirror

PAUL BEATTY
Joker, Joker, Deuce

JOSHUA BENNETT
Owed
The Sobbing School

TED BERRIGAN
The Sonnets

LAUREN BERRY
The Lifting Dress

JOE BONOMO
Installations

PHILIP BOOTH
Lifelines: Selected Poems 1950–1999
Selves

JIM CARROLL
Fear of Dreaming: The Selected Poems
Living at the Movies
Void of Course

ALISON HAWTHORNE DEMING
Genius Loci
Rope
Stairway to Heaven

CARL DENNIS
Another Reason
Callings
New and Selected Poems 1974–2004
Night School
Practical Gods
Ranking the Wishes
Unknown Friends

DIANE DI PRIMA
Loba

STUART DISCHELL
Backwards Days
Dig Safe

STEPHEN DOBYNS
Velocities: New and Selected Poems: 1966–1992

EDWARD DORN
Way More West

HEID E. ERDRICH
Little Big Bully

ROGER FANNING
The Middle Ages

ADAM FOULDS
The Broken Word: An Epic Poem of the British Empire in Kenya, and the Mau Mau Uprising Against It

CARRIE FOUNTAIN
Burn Lake
Instant Winner
The Life

AMY GERSTLER
Dearest Creature
Ghost Girl
Index of Women
Medicine
Nerve Storm
Scattered at Sea

EUGENE GLORIA
Drivers at the Short-Time Motel
Hoodlum Birds
My Favorite Warlord
Sightseer in This Killing City

DEBORA GREGER
By Herself
Desert Fathers, Uranium Daughters
God
In Darwin's Room
Men, Women, and Ghosts
Western Art

TERRANCE HAYES
American Sonnets for My Past and Future Assassin
Hip Logic
How to Be Drawn
Lighthead
Wind in a Box

NATHAN HOKS
The Narrow Circle

ROBERT HUNTER
Sentinel and Other Poems

MARY KARR
Viper Rum

WILLIAM KECKLER
Sanskrit of the Body

JACK KEROUAC
Book of Blues
Book of Haikus
Book of Sketches

JOANNA KLINK
Circadian
Excerpts from a Secret Prophecy
The Nightfields
Raptus

JOANNE KYGER
As Ever: Selected Poems

ANN LAUTERBACH
Hum
If in Time: Selected Poems, 1975–2000
On a Stair
Or to Begin Again
Spell
Under the Sign

CORINNE LEE
Plenty
Pyx

PHILLIS LEVIN
May Day
Mercury
Mr. Memory & Other Poems

PENGUIN POETS

PATRICIA LOCKWOOD
Motherland Fatherland Homelandsexuals

WILLIAM LOGAN
Macbeth in Venice
Madame X
Rift of Light
Strange Flesh
The Whispering Gallery

J. MICHAEL MARTINEZ
Museum of the Americas

ADRIAN MATEJKA
The Big Smoke
Map to the Stars
Mixology

MICHAEL MCCLURE
Huge Dreams: San Francisco and Beat Poems

ROSE MCLARNEY
Forage
Its Day Being Gone

DAVID MELTZER
David's Copy: The Selected Poems of David Meltzer

ROBERT MORGAN
Dark Energy
Terroir

CAROL MUSKE-DUKES
Blue Rose
An Octave Above Thunder: New and Selected Poems
Red Trousseau
Twin Cities

ALICE NOTLEY
Certain Magical Acts
Culture of One
The Descent of Alette
Disobedience
For the Ride
In the Pines
Mysteries of Small Houses

WILLIE PERDOMO
The Crazy Bunch
The Essential Hits of Shorty Bon Bon

DANIEL POPPICK
Fear of Description

LIA PURPURA
It Shouldn't Have Been Beautiful

LAWRENCE RAAB
The History of Forgetting
Visible Signs: New and Selected Poems

BARBARA RAS
The Last Skin
One Hidden Stuff

MICHAEL ROBBINS
Alien vs. Predator
The Second Sex

PATTIANN ROGERS
Generations
Holy Heathen Rhapsody
Quickening Fields
Wayfare

SAM SAX
Madness

ROBYN SCHIFF
A Woman of Property

WILLIAM STOBB
Absentia
Nervous Systems

TRYFON TOLIDES
An Almost Pure Empty Walking

VINCENT TORO
Tertulia

SARAH VAP
Viability

ANNE WALDMAN
Gossamurmur
Kill or Cure
Manatee/Humanity
Trickster Feminism

JAMES WELCH
Riding the Earthboy 40

PHILIP WHALEN
Overtime: Selected Poems

ROBERT WRIGLEY
Anatomy of Melancholy and Other Poems
Beautiful Country
Box
Earthly Meditations: New and Selected Poems
Lives of the Animals
Reign of Snakes

MARK YAKICH
The Importance of Peeling Potatoes in Ukraine
Spiritual Exercises
Unrelated Individuals Forming a Group Waiting to Cross